Photography

EXPRESS

Photography Express

Photography

EXPRESS

Know How to Get into Photography and
Become a Professional Photographer

Patrick Powers & KnowIt Express

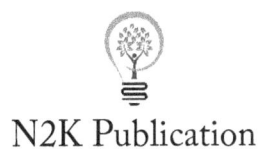

N2K Publication

ISBN 978-1-534-76903-8

Printed in the United States of America

First Edition

Welcome to the *Know It Express* - the express lane to knowledge!

To stay up-to-date, please be sure to sign up for **our newsletter** at http://www.KnowItExpress.com and follow us on social media:

https://www.facebook.com/KnowItExpress
https://twitter.com/KnowItExpress
https://plus.google.com/+KnowItExpress

Photography Express

EXPRESS LANE

Photography Express

CHAPTER 1

Capturing the Moment

Timeless Art

They say a picture is worth a thousand words, and in some cases...more than that.

Whether you want to capture a moment with friends, develop your artistic side, or make some money with your photos—then **photography** is right for you!

And the good news is, you don't even need a fancy camera! Sure, a decent camera has its advantages, but *ultimately* your own eye will determine the quality of the photograph.

Photography is an art and requires just as much creativity as painting, but in different ways. As with all arts, you can hone your skills. Just learning a few simple tricks will greatly improve your photography.

Even if you currently know nothing about photography, if you follow what will be discussed, you'll soon be a well-equipped, adept photographer.

So let's start exploring the skills, tricks, and art of photography.

Before We Begin

Now there is one very important thing you need to contemplate before we begin: what kind of photographer do you want to be?

This has nothing to do with whether you want to go into this as your profession or not. No, what you need to consider is what you want to take photos of primarily.

- Do you want to take portraits of people? Or of animals?

- Do you want to photograph fantastic landscapes in all their glory or do you want to capture the smallest of things close up?

- Do you enjoy taking many photos all at once? Or do you prefer taking your time to wait for the perfect shot?

Your answers to each of these questions will help you determine what equipment to purchase and what skills to hone as you strive to becoming an accomplished photographer.

Things To Keep In Mind Throughout

Here's a brief list of things to keep in mind while you hone your photography skills. Each one is brief and memorable with a quick explanation following it.

1.) A great camera will NOT make a great photo *unless* it's used by a great photographer. So don't use your money on the most expensive camera you can find. First; learn the craft and buy more expensive equipment as you need it.

2.) Beginners are absolutely capable of taking great photos *if* they have the passion. Once again, photography is an art. So if this is something you have an interest and passion for then you'll go far with it

3.) *Read the manual* for your camera, many times. You need to know everything about your equipment, so be sure to know the manual for your camera front to back.

4.) Take pictures of things you know or care about. Take time to think about what you want to photograph. It will help feed your passion.

5.) Don't try to learn everything at once! What we'll cover is a good head start, but there is always more that you could learn. For now, just focus on the basics. The rest you can pick up as you go along. Photography is essentially learning by doing.

6.) If you've just started, don't worry about building a portfolio. As you gain more experience you'll take better photos, so give yourself time to get better and don't worry about not having material. It'll come to you.

7.) Quality over quantity. Don't try to take as many photos as you possibly can. Especially at first, take the time to set up your photos so that you take as many excellent photos as possible.

8.) Take the time to study the work of photography masters. If you don't know where to start, check out artists such as Margaret Bourke-White, Alfred Stieglitz, Man Ray, Paul Strand, Henri Cartier-Bresson, Ansel Adams, and Edward Weston.

9.) Great photographs are about feelings as much as anything else. Think about the mood that you want to set with your photos and set up your subjects accordingly.

10.) Remember, your first 10,000 photographs will be your absolute worst! It's ok to be a beginner. Just keep at it and you'll be an expert in no time.

CHAPTER 2

Selecting the Camera

A Photographer's Baby

When getting a new camera, the most important thing to consider is what you want to use it for.

Different cameras come equipped for various specialty uses. Our advice is to get a good camera with standard capabilities as a base, and then build on to that camera with attachments as you need them.

Now our advice for all the absolute beginners is to start with the camera you already have, whether on your phone or a cheap disposable camera (it may be old fashioned, but the basics are the same). These cameras probably aren't what you thought you'd be starting with, and they won't be what you end up using. But you'll be much better off using the camera on your phone, or one that only cost you a few dollars, while you get the hang of taking photos and before you invest in a more expensive camera.

What if you decide that photography isn't your thing? Well, there you go; hence, start with something small and move on from there. This will also give you more time to figure out what kind of photography appeals to you the most and in what situations you like taking pictures. So when it's time to buy a better camera, you'll be armed with more information!

If you know that photography is what you want to pursue—or perhaps you've always like taking pictures and have finally decided to get serious about it—here are suggestions on what to look for when buying a new camera.

This is not a list of the best cameras out there: there are so many different brands and builds of cameras and they change each year, making it a "Top Ten" list less than helpful. Instead, consider what you should look for. We'll stick to what generally makes a good camera and then point you to websites that can help narrow down a specific choice for you.

Pretty much everyone uses a digital camera these days, so that's what we'll discuss here. Older style cameras that use film are still available but are really only used for hobby or niche purposes.

Camera Criteria Checklist

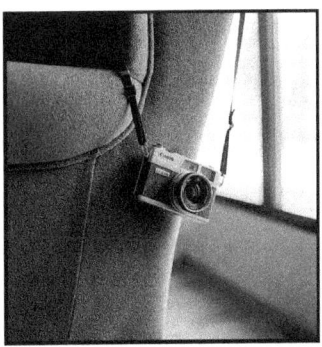

When you're looking for a new digital camera, there are certain things you want to look for in its capabilities, weaknesses, and strengths. Here's a checklist of sorts to help you consider carefully before you buy.

1.) **Don't overspend** - This is hugely important, especially because many people forget this one. DO NOT let yourself think that the most expensive camera is the necessarily the one you should get. Go for something decent that is within your budget, and don't feel the need to go past that budget. There are plenty of good cameras out there. One of them will fit your needs for a price that's within your range.

2.) **Pick a camera that feels right** - Okay, so this sounds like something out of fiction—"the wand chooses the wizard!"—but there's actually truth to it. Most importantly, you should pick a camera that feels comfortable in your hands and against your face. You should feel like the camera is an extension of your eye.

Consider the shape, size, and weight, keeping in mind that you'll want to be carrying it around a lot. It's not necessarily worth paying for an expensive camera that's so heavy that you never want to bring it with you!

3.) **Do your research** - Be sure to do some quick research on the brands and retailers you're considering. Knowing more about the manufacturer and the specifics of the cameras could prove invaluable. When you actually go to buy the camera, you'll know what to look out for.

4.) **Test the ISO range** - ISO (short for International Standards Organization) is a term for a camera's sensitivity, or how much light its sensor can pick up. The greater the ISO range, the more capable the camera will be in low-light situations. So you'll want a camera with a good ISO range. But be careful; even if a camera has a great ISO range, the noise levels (or bigger pixilation) might become unacceptable at certain levels. Keep in mind that just because a camera says it has a great ISO range doesn't mean it will perform well throughout that range. Take some time to examine the camera's effectiveness through its entire ISO range.

5.) **Test the sweet spot of the lens** - This is similar to the last point in that just because a camera lens says it has a certain zoom range doesn't mean it always takes a clear picture at any point in that range. The inner limits of that range, where the camera takes the clearest pictures, are what photographers refer to as the sweet spot. So again, test it out.

6.) **Don't over think megapixels** - It's easy to get caught up in the advertising of cameras, particularly in the definition or megapixels, but more isn't always better. Most pros will tell you that megapixels (the amount of microscopic dots in a photo) are vastly overrated. At the low end of the range, you'll notice the lack of clarity if you try to crop your picture or print it in a large size. Towards the high end, the differences are negligible, so it's not necessarily worth paying for extra once you have "good enough." To start, you'll be fine with a camera that shoots anywhere from 5-10 MP.

7.) **Know the flash capabilities and setting adjustment** - Flash will be important if you plan to do a lot of shooting inside. Flash comes standard in most basic digital cameras today, but the functionalities may differ from model to model. So when considering a new camera, consider its flash capabilities and be sure to learn how to adjust them for different lighting situations. If you plan on shooting in a variety of situations, rather than a fixed-studio setting, you'll likely want the settings to be easily adjusted without having to scroll through menus.

8.) **Learn the sensor size** - While megapixels are overrated, the sensor size is actually very important and is related to the ISO (ISO is based on the sensor size). The sensor size can limit the quality of the photos you take with this camera and there is a good deal of variety in sensor size on the market. So when you go to buy a camera, do your research ahead of time or find someone reliable at the store to talk to about sensor size in the cameras that you're considering.

9.) **How well do the accessories work?** - This includes battery life, compatibility with a tripod, ability to upgrade if necessary, etc. In other words, consider all the little things about the parts of your camera that don't directly relate to how well it takes photos. These are things to consider after you've found a camera that has the capabilities you need. Along these lines, realize that many camera accessories—including lenses—are specific to the brand, so your decision now may affect your future decisions about cameras and accessories. This is why many photographers are die-hard Nikon or Canon users.

10.) **If you end up not liking it, return it** - A camera is a significant investment—even the less expensive digital cameras on the market can cost a couple hundred dollars—so you want to get one that you like and that works well for you. If you make a purchase and later decide that it wasn't the right choice, don't be afraid to return it so you can get one that does fit you.

That should be enough to get you started! After using this checklist just once, you'll be an expert at navigating the market for your photography needs.

Choose Right Camera Over Best Camera

If you want to research cameras before you leave for the store, CNET, PCMag, TechRadar, and Digital Trends all have good websites with trustworthy reviews on the latest in photography technology. Think long-term here because there will always be a better camera coming out each year; hence, don't be like those folks who buy a new smartphone yearly just to get the latest model when their current one works fine.

Once you have your tools ready, you'll be able to start your work towards becoming an amazing photographer.

Now let's begin learning how to take fantastic photos!

CHAPTER 3

Mastering Photo-Taking Techniques

Composition

Now that you have a camera, it's time to start using it!

You may remember that we said being the best photographer doesn't mean having the best camera on the market. If you want to be good at this craft, you have to understand the basics of how photography works. So we'll break it down step by step.

Here's a quick exercise: identify the subject of each of these photos. Go ahead!

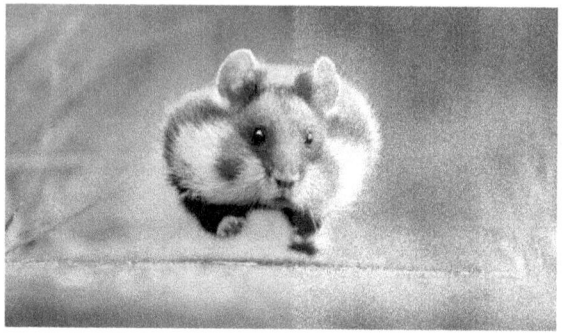

Subject:

_____

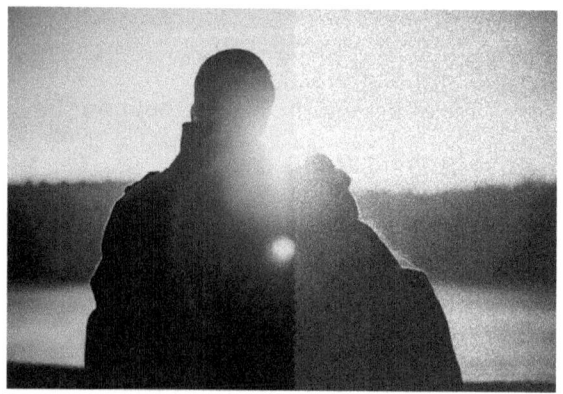

Subject:

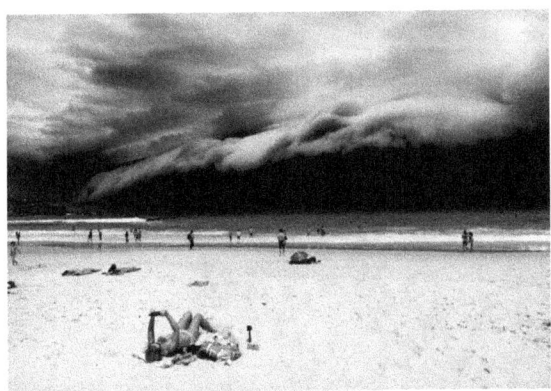

Subject:

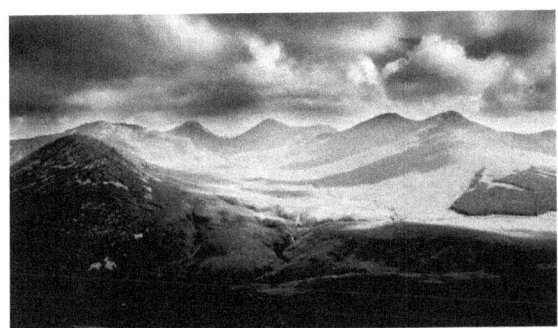

Subject:

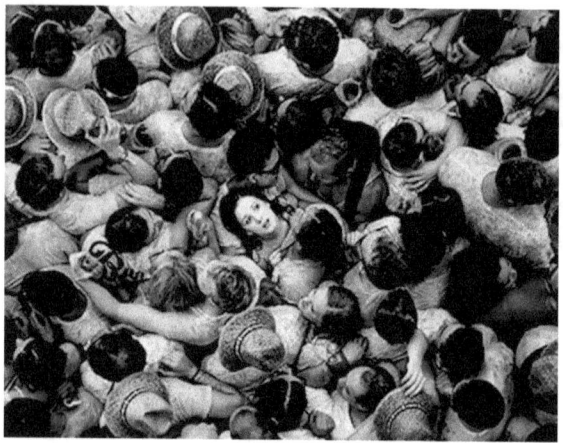

Subject:

Focus And Frames

How do you think you did? It probably wasn't hard.

If a photographer has done their job right, it shouldn't be too difficult to identify the subject of their photos because it will be whatever **draws the eye** towards it.

When you first look at a photo, whatever catches your eye immediately should be the intended subject. The subject might be big and obvious or small and obscured, but a good photographer knows how to make their subject clear at first glance, regardless of circumstances.

There are two keys to this: focus and framing.

- **Focus** is easy. Make sure that the camera focuses <u>on the subject</u>. Not something in the background. Not something in the foreground. Sometimes this requires repositioning so that the autofocus realizes what you want. This sounds simple—and indeed, it is—but one of the hallmarks or amateur photography is incorrect focus.

- **Properly framing** your subject is conceptually just as simple, but it takes a bit more practice to hone the skill. Now when we say frame, we're not talking about selecting a nice photo frame for your photos. Framing involves where the subject is placed within the photo.

Here's a visual example:

Well framed photo:

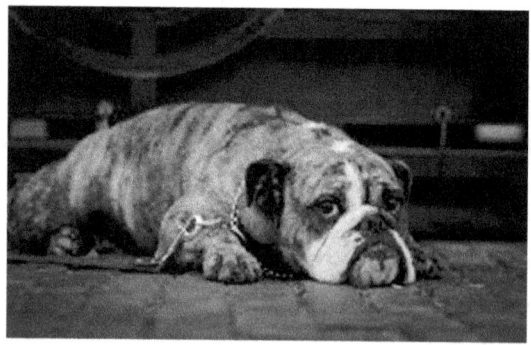

Poorly framed photo:

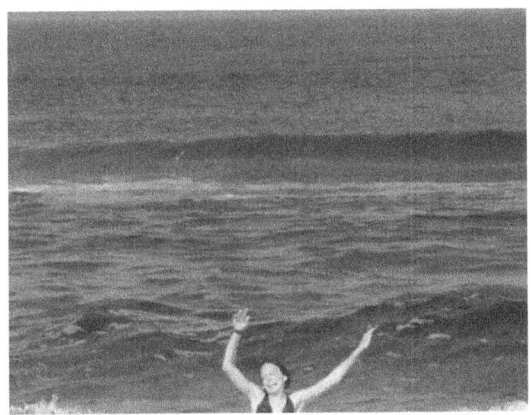

You can see the difference, right?

- In the first photo, it's clear what the subject is: the <u>dog</u> is set in the **center of the photo** and is framed by its surroundings. It stands out from the background.

- In the second picture, the subject isn't framed well at all. Yes, we can see that the <u>woman</u> was supposed to be the subject, but she's at the **bottom of the photo,** not central at all. And while she does stand out from the ocean background, there is an overwhelming amount of background, so it distracts from the intended subject.

The Rule Of Thirds

There's actually a rule that helps beginners with framing photos properly, it's usually taught very early on in any photography class and all pros know it well. It is the Rule of Thirds!

This rule divides photos into nine **pieces** using four lines going through the photo, dividing the picture into thirds both *horizontally* and *vertically*. Take a look at the examples below:

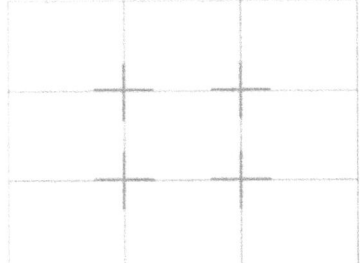 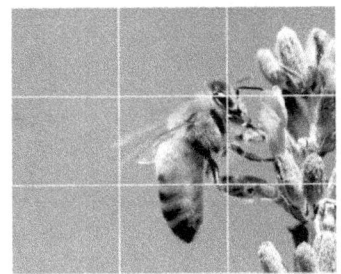

These lines are guidelines for where you want to place your points of interest (POI) based on where the viewer's eyes will go when they see your photo. Amateur photographers often put things smack-dab in the center of their photos. But the rule is to place your POI either *on the intersections of the lines* or *along the lines themselves.* This isn't arbitrary: studies have shown that humans are actually more likely to look along those lines than they are to look directly at the center of a photo.

In the example above, the bee's eye is the **point that will likely catch** your eye first. Then your eye will probably follow the body and the flower from there.

Here's another example:

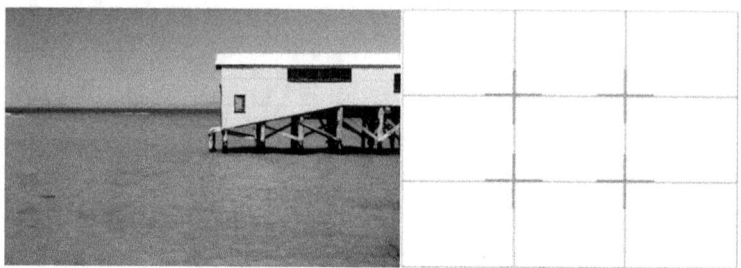

Notice that the <u>horizon</u> was positioned more or less *along one of the lines*.

In a landscape photo, this is usually the most effective placement for the horizon. In a portrait or group photo, faces should also be positioned along this line. NOT in the center—that leaves too much blank space at the top.

As you're beginning, use this rule until it becomes second nature to you.

But not all photos follow this rule of thirds. You can be creative with how you frame a photo and you should experiment. The rule exists because it is a very good guideline, so treat it as such. You should have a good reason to break it.

But that's still baby stuff, right? Anyone can tell a poorly framed photo from a well-framed one.

Now that we've covered the basics, let's learn some tricks of composition (how you set up and frame a photograph) that beginners often overlook.

Left To Right

It often pays to place your subject **towards the right side** of your photo.

Because most people *read from left to right*, that's typically the way your eyes travel when viewing a photo. Thus, when the subject is placed on the right of the photo it's more natural for a viewer to look past the negative space on the left to focus on the subject. This also gives the viewer a kind of satisfied feeling of completion.

If the subject is on the left side, viewers won't have taken in the rest of the picture and they'll often feel that the photo is incomplete.

Take a look at this example:

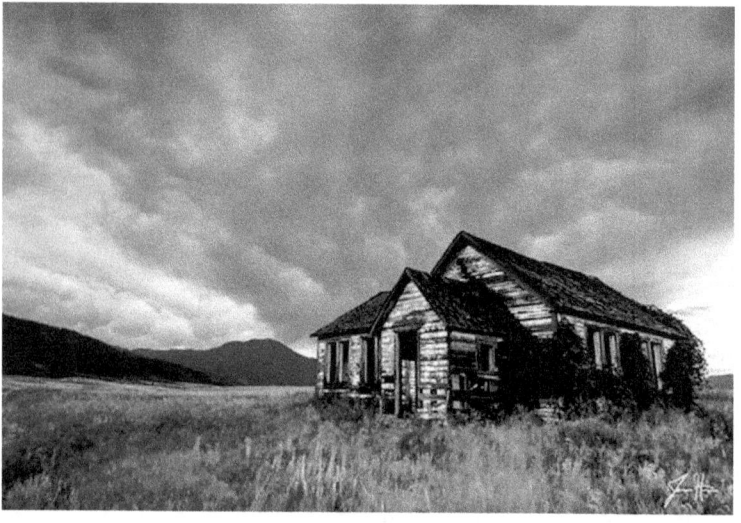

This technique is particularly useful if you really want your subject to stand out from the background. Of course this technique doesn't apply to every situation, and you have to work with what you've got. But, again, it's a good default.

Odd Vs. Even

Odd numbers are naturally more dynamically interesting than even numbers. It's not something we necessarily think about *but it's true.*

That's why **triangles** are aesthetically more interesting than **squares.** Triangles can be more dynamic while squares are comparatively boring and repetitive.

When photographing multiple objects, you'll want to have an odd number whenever possible.

Obviously, this won't always be the case and eventually you'll have to photograph an even number of objects or people. In those cases, use triangles in your composition to make it more dynamic.

Take a look at this example:

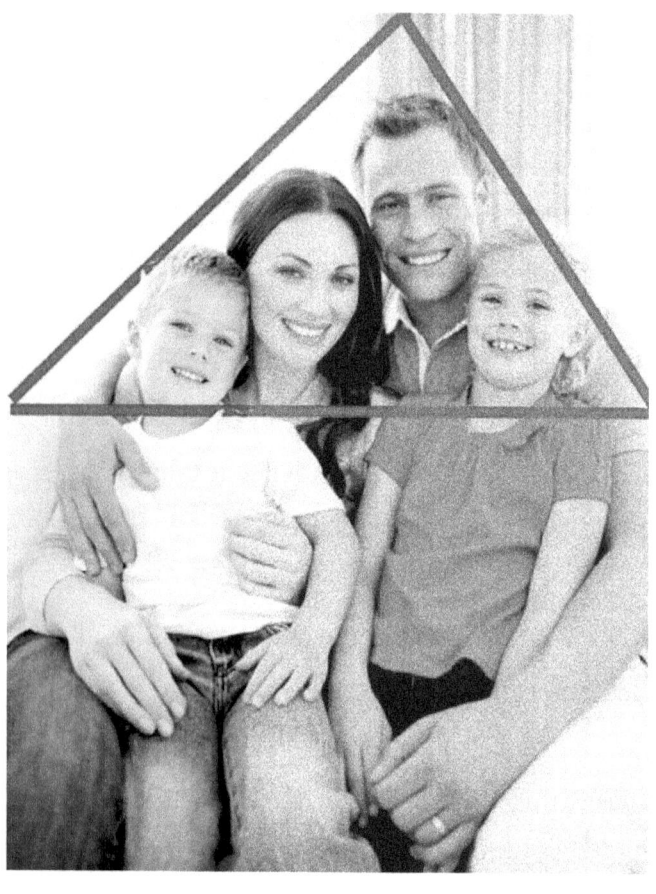

Notice that this family is positioned so that their faces form a triangle (of course, how could you miss it?). This *is*

tremendously more interesting than a photo of them standing in a **line**. There are, of course, situations where photographing people or objects in a line is the only viable approach, but when you can go for a more dynamic positioning.

Remember that you can do this in two ways: position the subjects or change your own angle on the scene.

Crop With Care

When setting up a photo or editing it, you may want to either zoom in or crop a little bit to focus in on the subject.

Say you're taking a photo of a man, and you want to focus primarily on his upper body. When you do this, be sure not to zoom or crop too much or too little.

A common mistake for beginners is to crop only a small part of the human subject, leaving an awkward photo.

- For example, a **full shot of a person** is often inadvertently cropped so that only the <u>feet</u> are missing, a viewer looking at this photo won't be looking at the <u>intended subject</u>, instead they'll be looking for the missing feet.

You'd be better off cropping the photo at the <u>waist</u>. This might take some experimenting, but you should get the hang of it after one or two poorly cropped photos. The principles of composition still hold, so use your eye to produce an evenly cropped, balanced, interesting photo.

Just remember, commit to your crops! Not too much and not too little.

Don't Bite Off More Than You Can Chew

Sometimes you may take a photo that simply has too much going on. If there are too many distractions in your photo, the **subject gets lost** and the **viewer becomes confused**.

When this happens, simply crop the photo down to a **smaller composition**: focus in on a smaller, more interesting scene.

This technique is most commonly used in landscapes, but it applies to portraits very well. <u>Full body shots</u> are very *difficult to pull off.* Sometimes it's better to stick to a <u>simple headshot</u> or a view of just the <u>upper body</u>.

Here are some key points to remember when framing a photo:

- Make sure the intended subject is focal (but not exactly centered) or framed by the surrounding background.

- Choose a background that will make your subject stand out.

- Stick to the Rule of Thirds!

- Position your subject on the right.

- Keep your compositions interesting, dynamic, and focused.

CHAPTER 4

It's All About the Lighting

The Flash

The next thing you need to know, and this is a big one, is how to **light your photos**.

You'll want to start with a **camera that has a flash** and get used to that. Using the <u>camera's flash</u> is appropriate in situations where there is **less natural light**, like at *night* or *indoors*. Yet make sure that your flash is off in situations with enough light!

Once you've gotten the hang of a basic flash, if you want to do more professional camera work you can invest in other lights sources.

Here are a few different ways to light a portrait photo:

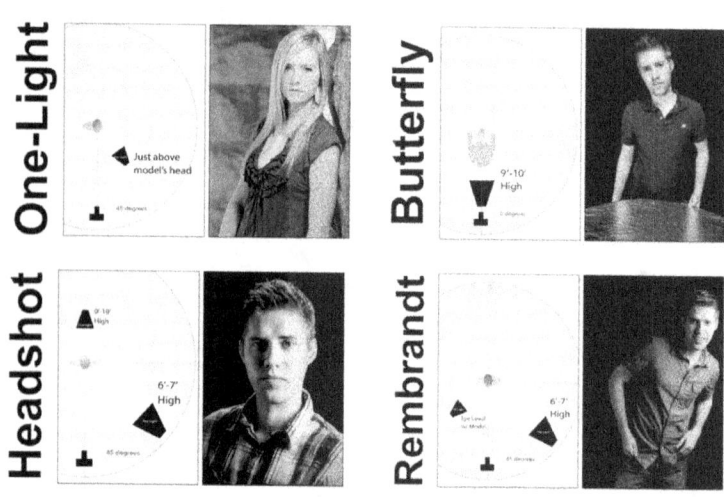

These simple lighting techniques are especially useful if you want to take up studio photography (although they can be used outside the studio as well).

You'll need to invest in some <u>simple lighting implements</u> such as **PAR cans**. Simple lighting implements are easy to find online or at stores like Wal-Mart.

Pay close attention to how each of these methods highlights the details of each subject. Each technique has a different effect, so you'll need to choose your lighting accordingly. You want to highlight the details of your subject without flooding them with too much light.

<u>Exercise</u>: Light IT Up

<u>Different subjects</u> will require **different approaches on lighting** because of each subjects' unique shape, color, and location.

The best way to know what you're doing with your lighting is to practice lighting on your own at home (but remember to try different lighting conditions, times of day, etc.). When you're in the field or at an event, you'll want to already know what to do so that you don't miss a great shot because you're fumbling around.

So here's an exercise that will help you become comfortable with your lighting options. You'll be using up to <u>two light sources</u> to photograph an object in your house (these light sources MUST be **artificial,** no natural light for this exercise).

Start by finding a dark room and bring your lights, camera, and object with you.

The key to this exercise will be experimenting with what is *not enough light* and what is *too much*.

- Too little light and you won't be able to make out the details of your subject (on the left, below).

- Too much light and your subject will be washed out (on the right, below).

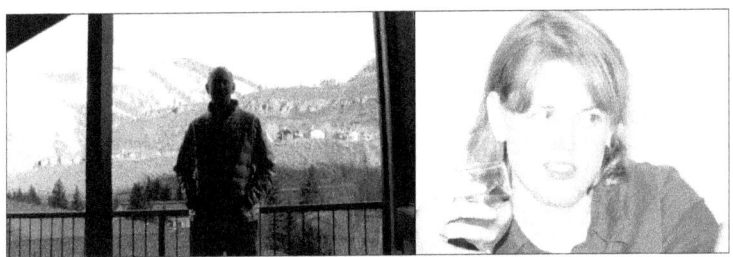

Ideally, your photos will resemble the <u>portraits</u> in the lighting examples, rather than these poorly lit ones.

It's always easy to say *what not to do* when it comes to lighting, but what should you actually do?

While you should experiment on your own, here are some <u>additional tips</u> that will give you a good head start on creating beautifully lit photographs.

Broad Lighting Vs. Narrow Lighting

This refers to the <u>width of the space</u> a light source casts light on.

- For example, a <u>flashlight</u> is purposefully built to be a **narrow light source,** to focus on where you point it, while <u>candlelight</u> is naturally a **broad light source** because a candle doesn't focus its light.

A broader light source will create **softer light,** while a more narrow light source creates a **harder light**. A broad light source will *lessen shadows and contrast* and suppress textures. A narrow light source, as you can probably image, *does the opposite.*

The type of lighting you'll want will depend on your subject and the ambient light. For <u>portraits</u>, you're usually better off using broader light sources.

<u>TIP</u>: The **further away a light source** is the **harder the light it gives off will be.** So move your <u>light sources</u> closer to <u>your subject</u> to create softer light.

Shadows Create Volume

Shadows aren't necessarily bad. You can actually use shadows to **create more volume** to your photo.

Lighting from the side, above, or below will **cast longer shadows** and ultimately make your photo **more dramatic, appearing three-dimensional.**

Here's an example of creative and effective shadows:

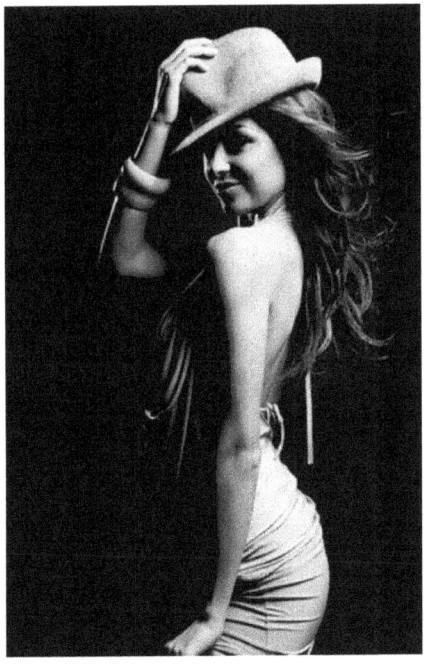

Light Has Color Even When It Appears Colorless

Remember that all light has color. Even though you may not pick up on it, your camera will.

Your camera measures what is called color temperature. Brighter, **more pronounced colors** are warm colors while **duller colors** are cool colors. You can adjust how the camera interprets this with the **white balance** settings.

When working with artificial lighting you'll typically want your subject to be comprised of warm colors and *contrast* that with a background of cooler colors.

Things to take away:

- Lighting is the most important aspect of setting up your photo. (So make sure the lighting is what you want before taking the photo.)

- Don't overexpose your subject.

- If you don't like the way your subject is lit, play with the lighting until you do.

- Use softer or harder lighting depending on what you want to focus on.

- Be creative!

CHAPTER 5

Polishing Photos with Post-Editing

Picture Perfection

Shooting photos is only one part of the job, however. You'll also need to edit your photos. Now some photographers edit a lot and some very little, but almost everyone edits some of their photos. So let's cover how to do so.

There are many different programs that you can use to edit digital photos (film is a lot more complicated and expensive). This is only the basics: it won't replace a tutorial with the software of your choice, but it'll help you think about the editing process, get your bearings, and consider your options.

What you do in <u>post</u> is just as important as *how you shoot your photos*. This will help you get the most out of your photos—whether you're perfecting that landscape to print and hang on your wall or optimizing a studio portrait for a paying client.

Now it is important to remember that any edits you make to a photo should be *minimal*. If you adjust something too much it could ruin the photo (not permanently, of course, because it's digital). A common mistake is to over process photos to the point that they look amazing...but fake.

Editing Options

Here's a list of the edits you should consider every time you edit a photo. If the shooting went well, you may be able to skip some of them, but you should always check!

1.) **Crop** - We've already covered this in terms of composition, but it's always best to check this when starting your edits. Even well-organized compositions might look a little bit better after some cropping. Experiment if you'd like, remember you can always press the **undo button.**

2.) **Remove any Sensor Dust** - We trust that you'll be a good camera owner and routinely clean the lens, but there's always the chance of dust or other debris getting on your lens or sensor. Unfortunately, even tiny flecks of dust will be noticeable at higher zoom levels or in areas that are comprised of a solid, pale color. Most photo editing software will have a "healing brush" or other tool to remedy this. You'll need to zoom in enough to visually scan the photo for any blemishes and remove them manually with the brush.

3.) **Adjust the Levels** - This refers to your lighting levels, as they affect brightness and contrast. Sometimes you'll get the exposure levels just right, but it's easy to be a little off, especially if you're outdoors in changing light. So try adjusting the levels manually in the software. There may be presets that could help you find the right balance for your composition.

4.) **Adjust the Saturation** - This refers to the temperature of the colors in your photo: the more saturated the colors are the brighter and warmer they will be and vice versa. More often than not, photos benefit from a little extra saturation. But it can be easy to overdo it (especially because the saturation tool is fun to mess with). Remember that going too far can make your photos look garish and over-processed.

5.) **Sharpen Up** - All photo-editing programs have a tool that sharpens details in your photo. They do this by pixelating the selected area just a little bit. Too much, however, can cause excessive and obvious pixelation. So use with care.

6.) **Convert to Black and White (optional)** - This is really just an aesthetic change, but monochrome photos are popular. Most photo-editing programs will have several other filters that you may wish to try. It can be surprising how changing the color scheme can alter the effect of a photo.

Photo-editing Programs

These sorts of basic edits are possible in any software. The particular program you use, however, will be unique in its interface and options (as well as other factors, including price). Naturally, you'll want to look into what software best fits your needs and budget, so we've gathered a list of the best brands out there to give you a place to start.

- **Adobe** - Even if you're not a photography enthusiast, you'll definitely have heard of Adobe Photoshop, a program so iconic that its name is often used to refer to any sort of photo editing. More than just a photo-editing software, it's also used for illustration and design purposes. Its creative capabilities as an editing software are unmatched, unfortunately so are its prices. However, if it's not in the budget to buy the full version of their latest version, there is also the option to rent the software with a subscription service on a monthly or annual basis. The same service is offered for Adobe Lightroom, their other premium photo-editing software. Photoshop Elements is the inexpensive and more user-friendly version, for those who may be a little intimidated by the vastness of Photoshop's advanced tools. Elements has most of the tools that Photoshop has but presents them in a way that's easier to grasp. Adobe products are known for their quality and reliability, so there's really no wrong answer when you go with them; yet if there is one downside is that the software can feel bloated and bulky at times with opening, saving, and loading.

- **Serif Affinity Pro** - Similar to Photoshop in capabilities, this software—exclusively for Mac users—has an arguably more intuitive interface. This is another alternative for those who may not understand Photoshop at first, however for those who do know Photoshop, will be able to use this program with great ease. With a price that easily beats its competition, it's hard to go wrong with this choice.

- **PhaseOne Capture One Pro 9** - This program rivals Adobe Lightroom in its capabilities, but it has a feature that other programs often don't. It creates a database that allows you to make edits and save your edited photos while automatically keeping the original photos intact. It also boasts a number of presets that surprisingly come out looking sharper and cleaner than most other preprogrammed presets.

- **MacPhun Creative Kit 2016** - This is another program only for Mac users. Despite the cheesy pun, it's a very capable piece of software. What's most is that it's incredibly user friendly and intuitive. If you've never used a photo-editing software before, this is an excellent option for you.

- **Cyberlink PhotoDirector 6 Ultra** - Another powerful alternative to Adobe products, much of PhotoDirector's interface and tools are influenced by Adobe Lightroom (so Adobe users should have no trouble adapting to this program). What PhotoDirector has that Lightroom doesn't, however, is an impressive number of effects that you can apply to your photo to achieve various means. These effects will create specific moods, doing much of the otherwise manual work for you and saving you time.

- **GIMPshop (free!)** - If all the above choices are out of the question due to your budget, GIMPshop is your answer. It's free and packs a punch with features rivaling Adobe Photoshop. However, if you plan to be a serious photographer, you should plan on eventually upgrading to one of the big boys. Due to the nature of free programs, updates aren't as frequent and currently on hold (because of an issue over the domain name gimpshop.com, which is registered and owned by a 3rd-party profiteer other than the original developer Scott Moschella, making it look like it's the official site). So if you're going to download this one, use the following link: https://sourceforge.net/projects/gimpshop.mirror/.

CHAPTER 6

Taking It to the Next Level in Becoming a Professional Photographer

Watchful Eye

In being a professional photographer, ALWAYS be sure to keep a watchful eye.

- This means observing your surroundings, constantly looking for the next great shot. Pay attention to lighting and think about ways to be creative with camera angles.

The best photographers are the ones who know when to take the best photos because they're always looking.

So feel free to bring your camera with you wherever you go. You never know what photographic or photogenic opportunities may occur.

Telling A Story

Think about what each of the following photos implies and the mood that it creates.

- What do you feel? What happened just before the photo? Just after?

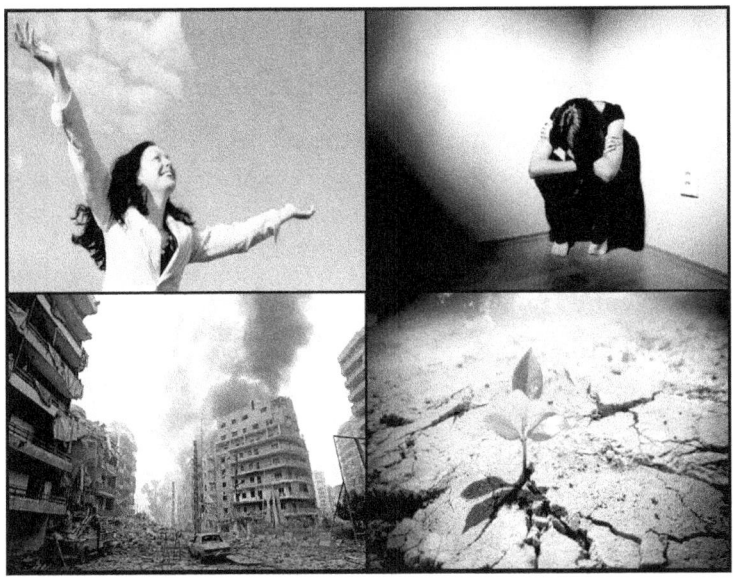

There are no wrong answers here.

The photographer often has a specific goal in mind when taking a photograph. Usually that goal is to **elicit some sort of emotional or subconscious mental response** in the viewer.

The subject itself creates some sort of response, but how the photo is set up can shape and amplify it. The photographer may choose to light the subject a certain way or frame the subject in a specific manner, and their choices will affect how viewers react to the photo.

Simply put, you want to create some kind of visceral response, and you need to use all of a photographer's tricks of the trade to do so.

<u>Exercise</u>: Mood Conjurer

For your last and final exercise, use what you've learned and try to create moods with your photos.

Take four photos that are particularly evocative. When someone looks at your photos, the mood should be immediate and undeniable.

Experiment with the following moods: happiness, anger, chaos, and peace.

Use all of your techniques, play with camera angles and lighting, and don't settle until you're happy.

If your intent is to take up photography as a profession, you need to be able to calibrate every time in order to get a final decent product.

Starting Your Own Photography Business

If you're serious about photography as a profession, you'll need to start your own business. (There's lots of other information out there for figuring out the logistics of starting any business.)

The following are things you'll want to know specifically to get your photography business off the ground.

- **You Need A Good Website** - You need a website not only to advertise your photos, but to advertise you. The website needs to be user-friendly and well organized, as well as aesthetically pleasing. A good resource is Squarespace. There are five very specific things you'll need on this website. 1.) Use the **home page** as a portfolio, and put your twenty best photos there so that's what people see first. 2.) Post the **specifications of your sessions** and your **prices**. 3.) You need a **brief bio page** about your professional work, yourself, and your photography style. 4.) A **blog section** will allow you to share stories about different sessions as well as ten or so photos from each sessions. And 5.) You'll need a **customer feedback section** so that other potential customers can see those (hopefully positive) reviews.

- **Use Email and Social Media** - These days most businesses have a **social media page** along with their own **website**. It's a great way to advertise to many people at once and it expands your potential clientele. Using email is definitely the most efficient way to communicate with your customers.

- **Think About Timing** - When advertising your business you'll want to consider the **time of year**. As seasons change so does the <u>general mood</u> of the populace, so you'll want to present your customers with photographs that capture the <u>mood of the season</u>. This doesn't necessarily mean you have to advertise with landscapes, but instead that the compositions you present on your homepage need to **match the weather in temperature and mood**. So in the **winter** you'll want photos with <u>cooler colors</u> and a <u>bit more shadows</u> while in the **spring** you'll want <u>warmer colors</u> and <u>more energetic scenes</u>. If you have particular holiday-themed photos, use those at the appropriate time (remembering to plan ahead, since Christmas photos, for example, are taken *before* Christmas).

- **Know How to Write to Your Customers** - When advertising, you'll want to grab a customer's attention with a line like "**Reserve Your Portrait Time for the Spring!**" and elaborate on that by giving them a <u>brief sales pitch</u> on what your session would be like. Then give them the <u>dates</u> you have *available* and follow with ways they can *contact* you. When emailing your customers you'll want to start by thanking them for coming to you, congratulate them/comment on the occasion that brings them to you, and get the details of the session (as in when and where). End by thanking them again, saying something like "looking forward to our session!" Above all, maintain a **positive attitude**. Keeping a good relationship with customers is key to starting a business. Those customers will likely refer others to you and help your business grow.

- **Don't Charge Too Much At the Beginning** - When you're starting off, keep your prices low, perhaps <u>$50 for 30 minutes</u>. You'll quite possibly be in the red at first, but you'll need to keep your prices low for at least the first few months so you can get prospects interested in your business. Once you've gained a substantial clientele, you can raise your prices.

- **Give Them All the Photos** - When you're starting off, it's much easier to give customers <u>all of the photos</u> you took (deleting any that are out of focus or aesthetically off, of course). We know that many pros <u>charge per photo</u> and only provide a few at most, but when you're starting you'll be better off just giving your customers all of the photos. It's what they want anyway and that'll boost their opinion of your business, which will help you grow more.

CHAPTER 7

Letting the Camera Shine

Tip Of The Iceberg

It's safe to say by now that we've covered a lot of ground, but remember this is only the beginning of you becoming a photographer.

You are stepping into a world of art. Keep exposing yourself to new techniques and other artists so that you're constantly growing as a photographer.

There is still so much more that you can learn about photography. We encourage you to never stop perfecting your skills!

Now that you have the basics down, you should be ready to start on your own and take your photography skills to even greater level.

Final Takeaway

Here are some key points to remember:

- The photographer makes a good photo, not the camera. The camera is only as good as the photographer.

- When buying a new camera, think about what you need long-term, don't just go for the most expensive one. The best ranking camera today probably won't be the best next year, and in the meantime, it might not be worth the cost.

- Know how to frame your subjects with intent. Apply the Rule of Thirds, Left to Right, and Odd vs. Even techniques.

- Lighting. Is. Everything. Experiment with different lightings at home, both inside and outside.

- Create moods and stories with your photos. They are your art. Make it expressive and emotional.

- Above all, be watchful. Make it a part of you. You never know when and where you'll find your next muse.

Maintain your passion for photography and drive yourself to be creative. Always look for new ways to capture subjects and create challenges for yourself. Don't settle for the same boring shots day after day, year after year. Experiment. Learn. Create.

You'll be taking great photos in no time! Have fun with it!

Photography Express

Photography Express

Now You Know!

We have now gone from - *NOT knowing*...to *KNOWING*.

Doesn't it feel great? As cliché as the proverbial saying goes: knowledge is, indeed, power. The more you know, the more empowered you become. Not knowing is defeating, as you succumb to feelings of helplessness and surrendering of your own self.

Of course, acquiring knowledge is a never-ending quest. There is a great saying by Nobel Prize French author Andre Gide: "Believe those who are seeking the truth. Doubt those who find it."

At the very least, we hope we have set you off in the right path in regards to what you have set out to know, and that you have enjoyed our little journey together for the time you have spent with us.

If you can tell us how we did, that would be very appreciated! We value your feedback and always look forward to hearing from you, or if there is any way we could improve the entire experience for you. If you have a success story, even better - please let us know!

http://www.KnowItExpress.com

Don't forget to stay in contact for we would love to connect with you.

https://www.facebook.com/KnowItExpress
https://twitter.com/KnowItExpress
https://plus.google.com/+KnowItExpress

What would you like to know? Let us know!

CONTACT US

Now onward for more power to you, and thank you!

Photography Express

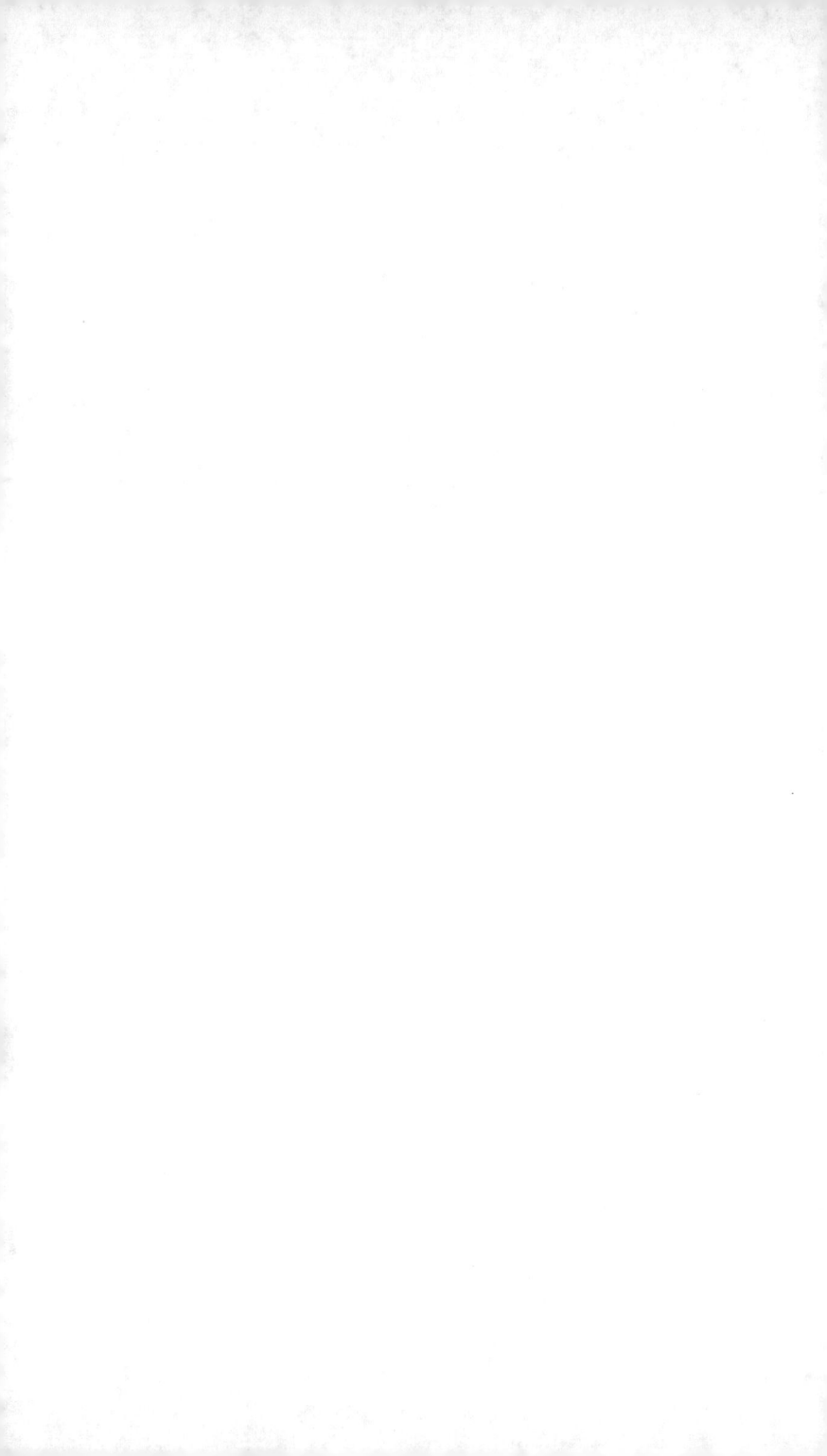